So Sue Me!

S. Harris

RUTGERS UNIVERSITY PRESS
New Brunswick, New Jersey

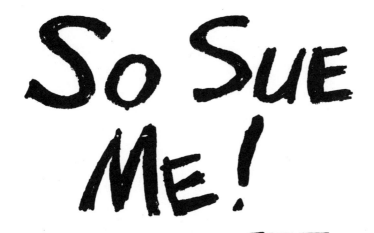

So Sue Me!

Cartoons on the Law
Sidney Harris

Most of the cartoons in this book have been previously published and copyrighted by the following publications: *Chicago Magazine, Discover, National Law Journal, The New Yorker, Playboy, Science, Trial Diplomacy Journal, The Wall Street Journal, Washingtonian,* and several publications of the American Bar Association.

Library of Congress Cataloging-in-Publication Data

Harris, Sidney
    So sue me! : cartoons on the law / Sidney Harris
       p. cm.
    ISBN 0-8135-1964-0
    1. Law—Caricatures and cartoons. 2. American wit and humor.
Pictorial. I. Title.
NC1429.H33315A4   1993
741.5'973—dc20   93-9215
                           CIP

British Cataloging-in-Publication information available

FOR KATHERINE,
MY LEFT-HAND WOMAN

So Sue Me!

1

"IF CERTAIN SITUATIONS AREN'T RECTIFIED BY THE END OF THE MONTH, WE'LL FORM A STEERING COMMITTEE THAT WILL FILE A FORMAL PROTEST WITH THE STATE PENAL SYSTEM. PASS IT ON."

"NOW WASN'T THAT NICE? WE TALKED, WE AGREED ON SOME THINGS, WE DISAGREED ON SOME THINGS, AND NO ONE THREATENED TO SUE ANYBODY."

4

"EVEN THOUGH THE EVIDENCE MAY LEAN IN THEIR FAVOR, I'M GOING TO VOTE AGAINST AMALGAMATED REFINING FOR ONE SIMPLE REASON: BAD VIBES."

5

"I BELIEVE YOU'RE MAKING A BIG MISTAKE GETTING INVOLVED IN AN EMBEZZLEMENT. GOVERNORS JUST DON'T DEAL IN EMBEZZLEMENT. GOVERNORS TAKE BRIBES."

"THE WITNESS HAS BARKED, MEOWED AND GIVEN US FIVE MINUTES OF BABY TALK. I'D SAY HYPNOSIS IS NOT THE ANSWER."

KELMAN & ROYSTON & 237 LESSER KNOWN BUT ALSO TOP-FLIGHT ATTORNEYS

8

"BUT IF WE DECRIMINALIZE MARIJUANA, WON'T WE HAVE TO CRIMINALIZE SOMETHING ELSE?"

"DO YOU SWEAR TO TELL YOUR VERSION OF THE TRUTH AS YOU PERCEIVE IT, CLOUDED PERHAPS BY THE PASSAGE OF TIME AND PRECONCEIVED NOTIONS?"

12

"MOST EXTREME CHANGE OF VENUE I'VE EVER HAD."

13

"As Dostoevsky said in 'Crime and Rehabilitation'..."

14

INEXPERT WITNESS

"APPARENTLY JEFFERSON DIDN'T SAY A <u>WORD</u> ABOUT DRUG TESTING."

"You should have signed a contract.
A high-five just isn't binding."

"SOMETIMES THERE'S LAW WITHOUT ORDER, AND SOMETIMES THERE'S ORDER WITHOUT LAW, BUT I NEVER SEEM TO SEE LAW AND ORDER TOGETHER ANYMORE."

19

"COUNSEL MAY OBJECT, BUT HE MAY NOT WHINE."

"THANKS TO US, EVERY DAY IS JUDGMENT DAY."

22

SUPREME COURT

COURT OF APPEALS

CRIMINAL COURT

DOMESTIC COURT

J. harris

COURTHOUSE MALL

23

"YES, I'M WELL AWARE OF MY RESPONSIBILITY TO THE COMMUNITY. THUS, I SPEAK IN CAREFULLY CONSTRUCTED SENTENCES, I LOOK SERIOUS AT ALL TIMES, AND I TRY MY UTMOST NEVER TO APPEAR TO BE A JERK."

24

"MY CLIENT ADMITS HE WASN'T INSANE AT THE TIME OF THE CRIME, BUT HE WAS VERY, VERY NEUROTIC."

PERPETRATOR OF A DARING, DAYLIGHT, ILLEGAL ELECTRONIC TRANSFER OF FUNDS, FLEEING THE SCENE OF THE CRIME

"I AGREE — THAT GENE DEFINITELY DOES <u>NOT</u> LOOK SPLICED."

27

"THE OPPORTUNITY TO BE FAIR AND JUST IS REWARDING — BUT WHAT I ESPECIALLY LIKE IS TAKING THE LAW INTO MY OWN HANDS."

29

"I WAS IN GOOD FORM TODAY —
OVERRULED SIXTY-SEVEN OBJECTIONS."

31

"WE'RE NOT SURE IF YOUR HUMAN RIGHTS HAVE BEEN VIOLATED, OR IF THERE HAS BEEN AN ABUSE OF POWER, BUT WE DO FEEL THAT, AFTER 7 YEARS, YOUR APARTMENT SHOULD BE PAINTED."

32

"WHAT IT COMES DOWN TO IS YOU SEEM TO
HAVE VIOLATED ALL TEN COMMANDMENTS, THE
FIRST TEN AMENDMENTS TO THE CONSTITUTION
AND THE U.N. CHARTER."

34

"GUILTY? I'D LIKE TO CALL IN A SECOND OPINION."

35

s.harris

36

"...AND AS YOU GO OUT INTO THE WORLD OF
INVESTMENT BANKING, THEATRICAL PRODUCTION,
BUSINESS MANAGEMENT, AND, YES, EVEN LAW..."

"FRANKLY, I'M DUBIOUS ABOUT AMALGAMATED SMELTING AND REFINING PLEADING INNOCENT TO THEIR ANTI-TRUST VIOLATION DUE TO INSANITY." 37

"MR. CUMMINGS WILL NOW DISCUSS THAT GRAY
AREA BETWEEN LEGAL ACTS AND ILLEGAL ACTS."

38

"AFTER MUCH DELIBERATION WE HAVE VOTED, 6-TO-3, NOT TO SAY 'CHEESE'."

39

40

"NOW I KNOW I'VE ARRIVED. THE COMPANY HAS BEEN ACCUSED OF AN ANTI-TRUST VIOLATION." 41

"WHEN IT'S 6-TO-3, YOU'RE ONE OF THE THREE. WHEN IT'S 7-TO-2, YOU'RE ONE OF THE TWO. WHEN IT'S 8-TO-1, YOU'RE THE ONE. SIR, YOU ARE AN INCORRIGIBLE SPOILSPORT."

42

"TRUE, THERE ARE NO-FAULT AUTO ACCIDENTS AND NO-FAULT DIVORCES, BUT WE DO NOT YET HAVE NO-FAULT ROBBERIES."

43

"IT DOESN'T MATTER THAT YOU'RE ONE OF THE LARGEST LAW FIRMS IN THE COUNTRY. ONLY ONE PERSON AT A TIME MAY QUESTION THE WITNESS." 45

"WE HAVE FORTY MILLION OF THEM, BUT FRANKLY THEY ALL LOOK ALIKE TO ME."

46

"SAY, WHAT ABOUT THE
NO-KNOCK LAW?"

IN CONGRESS, JULY 4, 1776.

The unanimous Declaration of the thirteen States of America

(Reading time: 7 minutes, 42 seconds)

S. Harris

49

"THE VOTE IS 16 TO 4. ONE OF YOU HAS VOTED TWELVE TIMES."

"MY CASE FELL APART WHEN MY LAWYER PLEADED THE SEVENTEENTH AMENDMENT— IT HAS TO DO WITH THE ELECTION OF SENATORS."

"SURE I'M A STRONG DEFENDER OF THE FIRST AMENDMENT AND ALL ITS RAMIFICATIONS, BUT IT'S VERY CLEAR THAT IF HE CALLED US A BUNCH OF JERKS, THAT'S LIBEL."

"DID YOU SAY 'BLIND'? I ALWAYS
THOUGHT JUSTICE WAS DEAF!"

53

"THE HECK WITH THE CONSTITUTION—
I'M GOING TO SHOUT 'FIRE'."

"I WANT THE MARBLES IN THIS BAG LABELLED EXHIBITS ONE THROUGH 237."

"MAYBE HE HAS THE KEY."

"IS THE CONSTITUTION THE ONE THAT BEGINS
'WHEN IN THE COURSE OF HUMAN EVENTS',
OR IS IT THE ONE THAT BEGINS 'WE, THE
PEOPLE OF THE UNITED STATES, IN ORDER
TO FORM A MORE PERFECT UNION'?"

"WHAT DO YOU KNOW? YOU WERE ONLY A LAWYER. I WAS A JUDGE."

58

"BELIEVE ME, IT WASN'T EASY GETTING A JURY OF YOUR PEERS."

"QUOTAS IN SCHOOLS DON'T BOTHER ME, QUOTAS IN UNIONS DON'T BOTHER ME, QUOTAS IN INDUSTRY DON'T BOTHER ME. BUT A QUOTA HERE ON THE BENCH—— _THAT_ WOULD BOTHER ME."

61

"I THINK YOU DON'T QUITE UNDERSTAND THE ROLE OF PUBLIC DEFENDER."

THE SUPREME COURT PACING THE FLOOR TRYING TO REACH A TOUGH DECISION

"WE'RE NUMBER ONE! WE'RE NUMBER ONE!..."

65

"BASCOMBE HAD PUT ALL HIS ASSETS INTO A BLIND TRUST, BUT IT WAS SET UP SO WELL, HE CAN'T EVEN <u>LOCATE</u> IT."

EXPERT WITNESS IN THE FIELD OF EXPERT WITNESSES

"REMEMBER US? THE JURY YOU BRIBED TO LET YOU OFF..."

"...AND, IN SUMMATION, IF I AM FATED TO LOSE THIS DECISION, PLEASE DON'T MAKE IT NINE-ZIP."

69

NINTH INNING, BASES FILLED, TWO OUT...

"HAS THE JURY
REACHED A VERDICT?"

"HERE IT IS: 'ONE, TWO, THREE STRIKES YOU'RE OUT...' OOPS, WRONG CONSTITUTION."

73

"THE MESSAGE OF MY NEXT SONG IS THE
MESSAGE OF OUR RIGHTS AND FREEDOMS. I'M
GOING TO SING THE 7TH, 10TH, 19TH AND 24TH
AMENDMENTS TO THE CONSTITUTION."

"I THOUGHT PLEA-BARGAINING WAS SOMETHING ENTIRELY DIFFERENT."

"I'M PRETTY SURE I UNDERSTAND BREAKING AND ENTERING, AND ASSAULT— BUT I STILL HAVE A LOT OF TROUBLE SPOTTING THE REDEEMING SOCIAL VALUE IN BOOKS AND MOVIES."

"WE SAID, MADAM, THAT YOU MAY VIEW
PORNOGRAPHY IN THE PRIVACY OF YOUR HOME.
WE DIDN'T SAY YOU HAD TO!"

77

"THIS CASE REMINDS ME OF ATKINS V. MISSOURI, LEVELTON V. THE RICHARDSON CORP. AND MUHAMMAD ALI V. JOE FRAZIER."

78

"DO WE LIST MONEY FROM STOLEN PROPERTY AS WAGES OR CAPITAL GAINS?"

"IT WAS MEDITATED, YOUR HONOR, BUT NOT PREMEDITATED."

80

"THE SUBJECT OF THE ESSAY IS 'WHY I DESERVE A LARGE AMOUNT OF MONEY', AND YOU WILL HAVE TO WRITE IT HERE AND NOW."

81

82 "HOW COME THE MINORITY OPINION, WHICH YOU WROTE YOURSELF, IS LONGER THAN THE MAJORITY OPINION, WHICH EIGHT OF US WROTE?"

"THIS IS PERFECTLY LEGAL. THEY'RE ONLY LIMITING OUR OUTSIDE INCOME FROM SPEECHES AND ARTICLES."

84

"THERE'LL BE A LOT OF CASES OF MISTAKEN IDENTITY TO CLEAR UP IF THEY EVER DO CATCH THE REAL CRIMINAL."

"IT WAS WORSE THAN OBSTRUCTING JUSTICE. HE MANAGED TO OBSTRUCT LIBERTY AND JUSTICE FOR ALL."

"WHO GETS PRECEDENCE—OUR LEGAL
DEPARTMENT OR OUR ETHICS COMMITTEE?"

87

"I KNOW YOU'RE LAW-ABIDING, FRED, BUT I'M SURE THE LEASH-LAW IS ONLY IN EFFECT OUTDOORS."

89

90

"IF WE'RE SO DAMN SUPREME, WHY AREN'T WE HAPPY?"

"JUST BETWEEN US, DILLON – HOW <u>DOES</u> A BILL BECOME A LAW?"

"THIS TRIAL HAS HAD A COURT-APPOINTED LAWYER AND A COURT-APPOINTED PSYCHIATRIST. NOW, FOR A CHANGE OF PACE, I'D LIKE TO INTRODUCE A COURT-APPOINTED STAND-UP COMIC."

"WHAT I FOUND WORSE THAN THE CONVICTION WAS THAT TWO WINOS, A DELIVERY BOY, THREE RECEPTIONISTS, A CUSTODIAN, A TICKET TAKER, A ZIPPER TESTER, TWO FILE CLERKS AND A FEATHER SALESMAN WERE CONSIDERED A JURY OF MY PEERS."

94

"OH, YEAH—I'M JUST AS
SUPREME AS YOU ARE!"

"YOUR HONOR, MY CLIENT WOULD LIKE TO EXPLAIN HOW A FINANCIAL INCENTIVE DIFFERS FROM A BRIBE."

97

"SOCRATES, YOU HAVE AN ANSWER FOR EVERYTHING. YOU CAN CONVINCE ANYONE OF ANYTHING AND YOU KNOW EVERYTHING. YOU OUGHT TO BECOME A LAWYER."

"FROM UP HERE, THEY ALL LOOK GUILTY."

100

"WE ALL SEND THE BAD GUYS TO JAIL, AND LET THE GOOD GUYS GO FREE. YOU HAVE TO HAVE SOMETHING EXTRA TO GET ON THE SUPREME COURT."

101

"IF YOU SETTLE OUT OF COURT, WOULD YOU SEND ME A LITTLE NOTE AND LET ME KNOW HOW IT TURNS OUT?"

"IT'S A GOOD TREND—THEY DECRIMINALIZED GAMBLING, THEY'RE TALKING ABOUT DECRIMINALIZING MARIJUANA, AND, EVENTUALLY, THEY'LL PROBABLY DECRIMINALIZE ROBBERY."

103

104

"FRANKLY, I SOMETIMES FORGET WHICH IS AN AMENDMENT AND WHICH IS A COMMANDMENT."

"WHAT IT CAME DOWN TO WAS THE JUDGE
INTERPRETED THE CONSTITUTION ONE WAY
AND I INTERPRETED IT ANOTHER WAY."

TRIAL OF A COMIC

I PLEAD GUILTY.

HOW GUILTY DO YOU PLEAD?

AS GUILTY AS A FOX SITTING ON A PILE OF CHICKEN BONES AND FEATHERS.

S. HARRIS

"I TAKE IT YOU'RE ALSO IN THE
FEDERAL WITNESS-PROTECTION PROGRAM."

109

"I ASK YOU, LADIES AND GENTLEMEN OF THE JURY, IF MY OPPONENT'S DRAMATIC GESTURES AREN'T MORE ARTIFICIAL THAN <u>MY</u> DRAMATIC GESTURES?"

110

"GO HOME! THE WORLD HAS ENOUGH STUFF! WE DON'T NEED ANY MORE!"

"IT LOOKS AS IF SMITHERS PACKAGING, VENDRELL ET AL. VS. MELROSE COUNTY WATER SUPPLY IS THE CLOSEST THING WE'LL GET ALL YEAR TO A CRIME OF PASSION."

"IF THERE WAS A TOUGH GUN CONTROL LAW, WE PROBABLY WOULDN'T HAVE GOTTEN OURSELVES INTO THIS MESS."

"I HAVE NOTHING AGAINST YOU PERSONALLY, BUT IF I LET YOU GO, I'D HAVE TO LET EVERY HOMICIDAL MANIAC GO."

"IT'S A TELEVISION FIRST—TWO COMMITTEES ARE INVESTIGATING EACH OTHER."

"LET'S TRY TO OVERTHROW SOME LAWS OF NATURE AND SEE HOW SUPREME WE REALLY ARE."

"IT'S NOTHING PERSONAL, PRESCOTT. IT'S JUST THAT A HIGHER COURT GETS A KICK OUT OF OVERRULING A LOWER COURT."

"THEY THINK THEY'RE BETTER THAN ANYONE SINCE EACH OF THEM HAD BAIL SET AT OVER $250,000."

"KICKBACKS, EMBEZZLEMENT, PRICE FIXING, BRIBERY... THIS IS AN EXTREMELY HIGH-CRIME AREA."

"WHAT I REALLY MISS IS NOT HAVING MY OWN GAVEL, AND NOT BEING ABLE TO SHOUT, 'ORDER IN THE COURT!'"

"I DON'T KNOW WHAT TO MAKE OF HIM — HE'S IN FOR SOMETHING CALLED 'VIOLATION OF THE ELECTRONIC FUNDS TRANSFER ACT.'"

"IT'S JUST THAT THERE ARE 120 LAWYERS IN THIS FIRM, AND 119 OF THEM ARE PARTNERS."

"HE SAID WE SHOULD START WITHOUT HIM, AND THAT IF ANY VOTES COME UP, HE'S IN FAVOR OF PERSONAL FREEDOM, NATURE AND THE COMMON MAN."

125

"AS IF THE ILLEGAL ALIEN PROBLEM ISN'T BAD ENOUGH ALREADY!"

"REMEMBER, IT'S GUYS LIKE YOU — THE SMALLTIME CROOKS, THE PUNKS, THE MISFITS OF SOCIETY — WHO ARE RESPONSIBLE FOR GUYS LIKE ME HAVING THESE GOOD JOBS."

"SURE, GENETIC FINGERPRINTING CAN PROVE SOMEONE'S INNOCENCE — BUT NOT IN A CASE OF STOCK FRAUD."

"WHAT CAN THEY DO TO US? IT'S ONLY OUR FIRST OFFENSE."

"IT'S JUDGES LIKE YOU WHO ARE RESPONSIBLE FOR THE OVERCROWDING IN PRISONS!"

"IT WOULD HELP, MR. KRAMER, IF YOUR PUBLIC DEFENDER WAS AN ATTORNEY."

"THERE'S A SALE DOWNTOWN ON BLACK ROBES. PASS IT ON."

133

"WE'LL CONTINUE THIS TOMORROW. I'M ON A WORK-RELEASE PROGRAM, AND I HAVE TO BE BACK IN MY CELL BY SIX O'CLOCK."

"MY IDEA OF A VACATION WOULD BE GOING DOWN TO SOME LOWER COURT AND HEARING A NICE, SCANDALOUS DIVORCE CASE."

"IT'S NOT A <u>GAME</u> CALLED 'ILLEGALLY TRANSFERRING FUNDS'. IT'S WHAT I'M <u>DOING</u>... ILLEGALLY TRANSFERRING FUNDS."

PLAGIARISM MEANS THAT YOU USE SOMEONE ELSE'S WORDS FOR PROFIT AND...ER...GAIN, AND YOU DECEITFULLY TRY-ATTEMPT-TO PASS THESE WORDS- THESE WRITINGS -OFF AS YOUR OWN.
WELL, I NEVER USE SOMEONE ELSE'S WORDS FOR PROFIT AND...ER...GAIN, AND DECEITFULLY TRY-ATTEMPT- TO PASS THESE WORDS- THESE WRITINGS-OFF AS MY OWN.
J. harris

"YOU MUST HAVE FAITH IN THE CONFIDENTIALITY OF THIS OFFICE. NOTHING YOU SAY HERE WILL EVER GO BEYOND THE DATABANK."

"I'M BEGINNING TO PREFER THE WITNESSES WHO CAN'T REMEMBER."

141

"I BEG YOUR PARDON, YOUNG MAN, BUT WE GIVE OUR <u>OWN</u> DISSENTING OPINIONS."

143

"OH, YEAH! THE DECISION OF WHICH JUDGE IS FINAL?"

"HE'S RIGHT. YOU SIT IN THE NEXT CHAIR BECAUSE I ALWAYS SIT TO YOUR RIGHT, THREE SEATS FROM THE END."